THE NATURE *of* KENSINGTON

| KENT LAKE SHORELINE |

HARBINGERS OF SPRING AFTER MARCH ICE STORM

THE NATURE *of* KENSINGTON

A PHOTOGRAPHIC PORTRAYAL

by TED NELSON

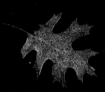

AUSTIN-CAROL PUBLISHING

AUSTIN-CAROL PUBLISHING
TEXT AND PHOTOGRAPHS COPYRIGHT ©1999 TED NELSON

CATALOGING-IN-PUBLICATION DATA
ISBN 0-9669880-0-0

Nelson, Ted
THE NATURE OF KENSINGTON: A PHOTOGRAPHIC PORTRAYAL
by TED NELSON.—Canton, MI :
AUSTIN-CAROL PUB., c1999.
p. cm.

ISBN 0-9669880-0-0
1. Natural history—Michigan—Kensington Metropolitan Park
   Pictorial works.
2. Kensington Metropolitan Park (Mich.)
   Pictorial works. I. Title.

QH105.M5 N45 1999   98-89962
508.774/3–dc21   CIP

Design by
JAMIE EVANS

Editing by
CAROL HENSON

Foreword by
CARL R. SAMS II & JEAN STOICK

Color Separations by
PRECISION COLOR
PLYMOUTH, MICHIGAN
1-800-222-6567

Printed and bound in Canada by
FRIESENS
ALTONA, MANITOBA

Published by
AUSTIN-CAROL PUBLISHING
CANTON, MICHIGAN

In loving memory of my Father and Mother

and with love to my daughters, Shelly and Becky

| Sandhill crane |

ACKNOWLEDGMENTS

With sincere gratitude, I recognize those whose shared spirit is reflected in the concept, design, and assembly of this book: Nancy, my wife and partner, for her steadfast love, loyalty, and courage. Chris Harris of British Columbia, Canada, for planting the seed from which this idea has grown. Bruce Montagne, for hours of brainstorming, organizing, and hard work. His contributions have been immeasurable. Carl R. Sams II and Jean Stoick, for their friendship and support of this project. Dan Goodenow for his friendship and technical guidance. My friends, Marilyn Kazmers and Roger Eriksson, because they were there when this idea was conceived, and for their expressed confidence in its success.

My family and many other friends who offer continued loyalty and support.

PRECISION COLOR
Innovative Imaging

Thank you Precision Color.
Your guidance and expertise
brought my book to life.

—Ted Nelson

| FOR ITS BROAD NOSE, NANCY AFFECTIONATELY DUBBED THIS WHITETAIL, "BUCK UGLY" |

GOLDENROD AND NARROW-LEAVED CATTAILS

FOREWORD

Because of its beauty and abundant wildlife, Kensington Metropolitan Park is one of our most treasured places. We discovered Kensington in 1982 during the early stages of our photographic careers. At that time, we came to know a few photographers who were already exploring the park and who shared with us many of its special secrets. Ted Nelson was one of those photographers. Today, we know him as a friend who shares our familiarity with Kensington and our love of its diverse, natural areas.

Throughout the years, we have come to recognize Ted's unique photographic style. A style that demonstrates the subtle placement of subject and a sensitive use of color and light to create compelling compositions. Ted brings the same creative eye to broad landscapes, intimate wildlife portraits, and captivating close-up images.

As wildlife photographers, we know the countless hours required to pull together a collection of photographs like those presented in "**THE NATURE *of* KENSINGTON**". In this book, we see vivid reflections of Ted's passion for the natural world and the jewel of the Metroparks…Kensington.

Carl R. Sams II & Jean Stoick

| ROSY MAPLE MOTH ON EVENING PRIMROSE |

INTRODUCTION

Beginning with its beautiful rolling landscape, Kensington Metropark is a place of extraordinary diversity. Various parts of this landscape, influenced differently by the physical elements of the environment, support different wildlife habitats. There are marshes, swamps, streams, lakes, meadows, temporary and permanent ponds, transitional and climax forests. Also, within each of these, are micro-habitats such as that formed by a fallen tree and between each, zones of gradual transition from one to the next. In turn, every habitat, micro-habitat, and transitional zone may be characterized by different and overlapping natural communities. Thus, the park boundaries encompass over 4,300 acres of diverse wildlife sanctuary.

| SUNDAY MORNING |

Such diversity contrasts sharply with the probable future of the lands surrounding Kensington. Its site, along the Interstate 96 corridor, in southeast lower Michigan, lies directly in the path of expanding development associated with the Metropolitan Detroit area. Development necessarily results in the destruction of wildlife habitat. It is estimated that, during a recent five year period, Metro Detroit's natural areas declined by roughly 40,000 acres! In most suburban Detroit communities, there is little or no wildlife habitat left, and the future looks grim for areas like those around Kensington that lie in the path of further development. Like the islands in its own Kent Lake, the future of Kensington Metropark and places like it, may be to stand as islands of natural diversity surrounded by developed communities. This, alone, is testimony to the value of this place.

While its significance as a wildlife sanctuary is apparent, for many visitors to the park, its value is much more personal. My sister-in-law, Bonnie, describes her memory as follows: "*I loved those early morning rides, especially when fog would settle over the water and meadows of Kensington. We wouldn't open our morning coffee until we were in the park, where we would drive slowly, looking for deer. Those mornings we shared were important to Tom and me. I think they brought us closer together.*" For some, Kensington is a place to gather socially. Others find a site for revitalizing, recreational activity. For me, there is value that comes from the opportunity for seclusion and intimacy with nature. Kensington is a place I can go for a kind of rejuvenation of the spirit; away from an increasingly aggressive society; away from the clamor and "road rage" that are daily realities of living in this part of the world. Inside the park and relaxed on a hilltop bench, I realize how my mood contrasts with that during my morning drive on the congested Interstate. I am calm. The seclusion allows quiet reflection. I am fully aware of the movement, humidity, and warmth of the air, the apparent texture of clouds, the autumn hues of grass, and seeds bursting from milkweed pods. This experience is important to me. My mind drifts back to my hunting days and the words of my long-time friend, Jeff Snarey. "*When I'm in the natural world and alone*" he would say, "*I am as close as I get to God.*" I am certain that for others, as well as me, there is spiritual value in a place like this.

In my case, this "connection" with nature is expressed through photography. Each photograph in this book represents a moment in time when natural elements like moisture, wind, and light, offer the opportunity to record an uncommon image. To recognize these moments requires the mood of solitude and quiet reflection that allows a keen awareness of the environment; a time when my mind is open, and my spirit is vulnerable. In this way, photography is an intimate, very personal endeavor. I offer the images in this book as my way of sharing the spirit of a few intimate encounters with the nature of Kensington Metropark.

WILDWING LAKE

MALLARDS

| Sycamore in autumn |

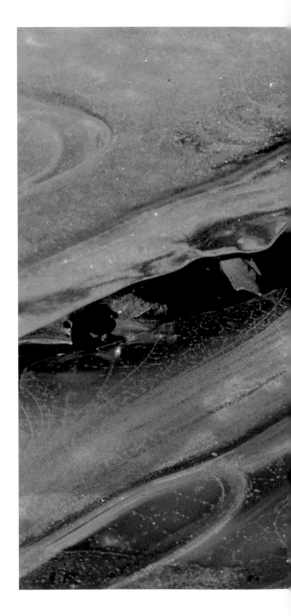

FROST COVERED LEAF SCAR AND SCULPTURED ICE

| Whitetail duos |

EARTH AND SKY

| M UTE SWAN |

Tufted titmouse – spring

DEPTFORD PINK AND FLOWERING SPURGE

| Wood duck drake |

| WHITETAIL DOE |

| Suspended in ice — dragonfly nymph and spring peeper |

| Redbud and flowering dogwood |

| Male cardinal |

| AT SUNRISE |

| BLACK-CAPPED CHICKADEE |

WHITE-BREASTED NUTHATCH

| RISING SUN SPOTLIGHTS DAMSELFLY |

| GRASSHOPPER EXOSKELETON ON DEPTFORD PINK |

| OAK LEAF IN ICE |

LOCUST AND WHITETAIL

| Fog settles in the meadow |

| FOG SETTLES OVER KENT LAKE |

| WHITETAIL BUCK AND DOES |

Curious whitetail and sandhill cranes

MEADOW AT FIRST LIGHT

MORNING FROST ON OAK LEAVES AND GOAT'S BEARD

MOODS OF THE MEADOW

A<small>MONG THE LATE SUMMER HUES OF LOVE GRASS</small>: B<small>UTTERFLY-WEED AND ASTERS</small>

MARSH MARIGOLD

| Patterns of ice and snow |

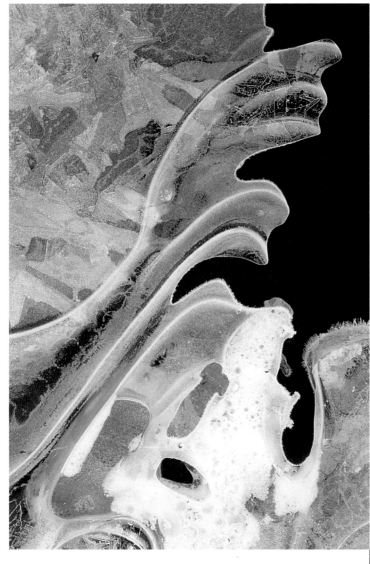

| CATTAIL MARSH AND CLIMAX FOREST |

| Rising sun |

| Grape leaf silhouettes |

WHITETAIL FAWN

| M U T E S W A N C Y G N E T S |

REFLECTIONS OF WINTER MORNINGS

HOARFROST ON OAK LEAF MARGINS

THE EDGE, WHERE ICE MEETS FLOWING WATER

EARLY BLOSSOM OF SKUNK CABBAGE AND LEAVES

| DEW COVERED LOVE GRASS AND DRAGONFLY |

WHITETAIL DOE AND WILD BERGAMOT

| The color of october |

| WINTER WHITETAIL |

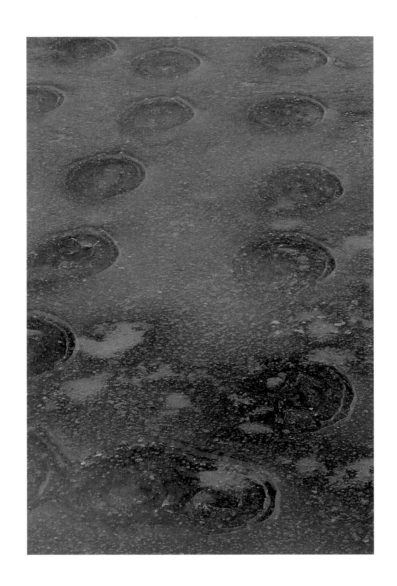

DISTORTED DEER TRACKS TRAVERSE A FROZEN POND

HERON ROOKERY

FEBRUARY MORNING

| REVELATIONS OF TRANSPARENT ICE |

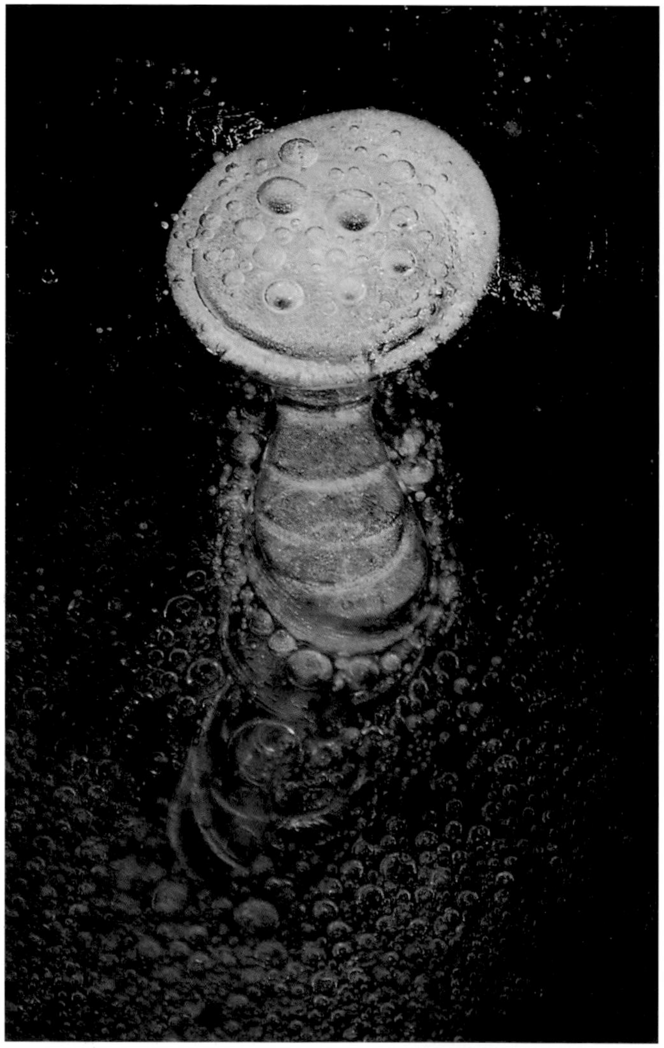

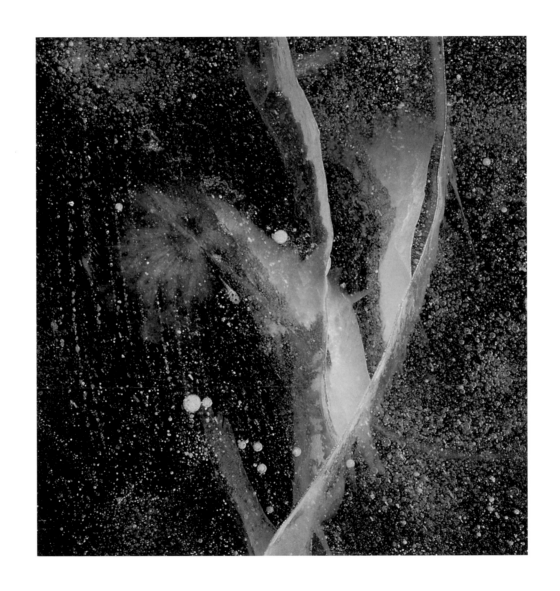

| RED SQUIRREL |

MALE DOWNEY WOODPECKER

SEPTEMBER MEADOW

| GOLDENROD |

| KILLDEER AT NEST |

| OLD OAK TREE |

| Mute swans in morning mist |

| Sᴀssᴀғʀᴀs |

| Sensitive fern |

THE NATURE *of* KENSINGTON

INQUIRIES REGARDING THIS BOOK SHOULD BE ADDRESSED TO:

AUSTIN-CAROL PUBLISHING
2018 LONE WOLF LANE
CANTON, MI 48188

TO ORDER BY PHONE, CALL 734-394-1261